TIPS AND GIST TO HELP YOU PAY YOUR HOMELOAN FASTER AND FINANCIAL FREEDOM

A PRACTICAL GUIDE TO OVERCOMING MORTGAGE HURDLES AN OWNING YOUR HOME

ROYCE BOATS

PREFACE

Hey there, fellow dreamer and homeowner-to-be! Welcome to the preface of a book that's about to change the game for you—yes, you! If you've ever felt the weight of your mortgage pressing down on your shoulders, if you've ever longed to break free from the shackles of debt and claim true financial freedom, then my friend, you're in the right place.

But before we dive headfirst into the treasure trove of tips, tricks, and nuggets of wisdom that await you within these pages, let me take a moment to introduce myself. I'm just your average Joe—okay, maybe slightly above average, but still just a regular guy—who, like you, once found himself staring down the barrel of a seemingly insurmountable mountain of debt.

But here's the thing—I refused to let that mountain crush my dreams. Instead, I rolled up my sleeves, dug deep into the trenches of financial know-how, and emerged victorious on the other side. And now, I'm here to share my hard-earned wisdom with you, dear reader, in the hopes that it will light the path to financial freedom for you too.

So, what exactly can you expect to find within the hallowed halls of this book? Well, let me give you a sneak peek. Picture it as your trusty roadmap—a roadmap that will guide you through the twists and turns of homeownership, helping you navigate the treacherous waters of mortgage payments with ease and confidence.

But this isn't your run-of-the-mill, snooze-inducing finance textbook—oh no. We're going to spice things up, infusing every chapter with a healthy dose of humor, wit, and yes, even a few cheesy jokes thrown in for good measure. After all, who said finance had to be dull and dreary? Not us!

So, without further ado, let's talk turkey—well, mortgage, to be more precise. We'll start by debunking some of the myths and misconceptions surrounding homeownership, setting the record straight once and for all. From there, we'll dive headfirst into the nitty-gritty of mortgage payments, exploring strategies to help you pay off your loan faster than you ever thought possible.

But wait, there's more! We'll also tackle the dreaded "B" word—budgeting—and show you how to whip your finances into shape like a boss. From cutting unnecessary expenses to boosting your income, we'll leave no stone unturned in our quest to help you achieve financial freedom.

And because we believe that knowledge is power, we'll arm you with all the tools and resources you need to succeed. From handy worksheets to interactive calculators, consider this book your one-stop shop for all things mortgage-related.

But perhaps most importantly, this book is a beacon of hope—a reminder that no matter how dire your financial situation may seem, there's always a light at the end of the tunnel. With a little bit of grit, determination, and a whole lot of elbow grease, you too can join the ranks of proud homeowners who have conquered their mortgages and reclaimed their freedom.

So, if you're ready to embark on a journey of financial empowerment, if you're ready to kiss your mortgage woes goodbye once and for all, then buckle up, my friend. The adventure of a lifetime awaits, and the key to unlocking its treasures lies within the pages of "UnlockTips and Gist to Help You Pay Your Home Loan Faster and Achieve Financial Freedom."

Are you ready to take the leap? Then let's dive in and discover the power of financial freedom together. After all, the journey may be long and winding, but the destination? Oh, it's worth every penny. Let's do this!

Table of Contents

This book is intended to provide general information and guidance on how to pay off your mortgage as soon as possible. The author and publisher are not engaged in

rendering legal, financial, or other professional advice. Readers are encouraged to seek the services of competent professionals in these fields if they require assistance.

While every effort has been made to ensure the accuracy and completeness of the information presented in this book, the author and publisher make no representations or warranties of any kind, express or implied, about the completeness, accuracy, reliability, suitability, or availability with respect to the content contained herein. Any reliance you place on such information is therefore strictly at your own risk.

The views expressed in this book are those of the author and do not necessarily reflect the views of the publisher.

Cover design by [RoyceBoats Publishing]

Published by [RoyceBoats]

Printed in [United States Of America USA]

First Printing: [March, 2024]

Introduction

Unlocking the Door to Financial Freedom

Welcome, dear reader, to the beginning of an exciting journey towards financial freedom and homeownership bliss. As you embark on this adventure with me, let's delve into the heart of the matter: paying off your home loan faster than you ever thought possible.

Picture this: You're sitting in your cozy living room, sipping a cup of coffee, and the weight of a mortgage hanging over your head suddenly feels lighter. That's the feeling we're chasing - the exhilaration of owning your home outright, free from the shackles of debt, and the peace of mind that comes with it.

But why pay off your home loan early, you might wonder? Well, my friend, there are countless reasons, and they all lead to one undeniable truth: financial freedom. Imagine the possibilities that open up when you no longer have to allocate a significant portion of your income towards mortgage payments. Traveling the world, pursuing your passions, investing in your future - the world becomes your oyster.

Now, let's address the elephant in the room - the daunting prospect of paying off your home loan ahead of schedule. It's no small feat, but trust me when I say it's entirely within your grasp. Throughout this journey, we'll navigate the winding paths of personal finance, uncovering hidden opportunities, and charting a course towards your ultimate goal.

But before we dive headfirst into the nitty-gritty details, let's take a moment to understand the landscape we're traversing. Owning a home is a significant milestone, a cornerstone of the American Dream, if you will. It symbolizes stability, security, and a place to call your own. However, for many, it also comes with a hefty price tag - the infamous mortgage.

A mortgage, while a necessary tool for most aspiring homeowners, can often feel like a heavy burden. The thought of decades of monthly payments looming over you can be overwhelming, to say the least. But fear not, for I'm here to tell you that there's light at the end of the tunnel, and it shines brightly with the promise of financial freedom.

In the chapters to come, we'll explore every facet of paying off your home loan fast, from maximizing your income streams to cultivating the discipline necessary for success. But first, let's dispel some common myths and misconceptions surrounding this journey.

Contrary to popular belief, paying off your home loan early is not reserved for the elite few or the exceptionally wealthy. It's a goal that anyone can achieve with the right mindset, strategies, and determination. Whether you're a recent graduate just starting your career or a seasoned professional nearing retirement, the principles outlined in this book are applicable to all.

But it's not just about the destination; it's about the journey itself. Along the way, you'll discover hidden talents, uncover new opportunities, and learn invaluable lessons about money management and personal finance. You'll develop resilience in the face of adversity, and you'll emerge stronger, wiser, and more empowered than ever before.

So, dear reader, are you ready to take the first step towards financial freedom? Are you prepared to seize control of your financial destiny and pave the way for a brighter future? If so, then buckle up, because we're about to embark on the ride of a lifetime.

In the words of Lao Tzu, "The journey of a thousand miles begins with a single step." Consider this book your first step towards a brighter, more prosperous future. Together, we'll turn your dreams of homeownership into a reality, one payment at a time. So let's roll up our sleeves, dive in headfirst, and make your journey towards financial freedom an unforgettable adventure.

CHAPTER 1

Understanding the Home Loan Journey: Navigating the Path to Ownership

Welcome, fellow adventurer, to the first leg of our journey towards financial freedom and homeownership bliss. As we embark on this thrilling expedition together, let's start by unraveling the intricate tapestry of the home loan journey.

Imagine yourself standing at the threshold of your dream home, keys in hand, heart brimming with excitement. But before we step across that threshold, let's take a moment to understand the terrain we're about to traverse.

The Importance of Homeownership

Owning a home is more than just a financial transaction; it's a symbol of stability, security, and a place to call your own. It's where memories are made, families are raised, and dreams take root. But for many, the path to homeownership is paved with challenges, chief among them - the home loan.

The Role of the Home Loan

A home loan, also known as a mortgage, is a financial instrument that enables individuals to purchase property by borrowing funds from a lender. It's a lifeline for aspiring homeowners, offering access to the housing market and the opportunity to turn dreams into reality. But like any tool, it comes with its own set of complexities and considerations.

Navigating the Mortgage Maze

Now, let's talk turkey - navigating the mortgage maze can be a daunting task. From interest rates to loan terms, there's a lot to wrap your head around. But fear not, for I'm here to guide you through the labyrinth and help you emerge victorious on the other side.

Understanding Interest Rates

One of the first hurdles you'll encounter on your home loan journey is navigating the world of interest rates. These seemingly innocuous numbers can have a significant impact on your overall mortgage experience, dictating everything from your monthly payments to the total cost of your loan.

Fixed vs. Adjustable Rate Mortgages

When it comes to interest rates, you'll typically encounter two main flavors - fixed-rate and adjustable-rate mortgages. A fixed-rate mortgage offers stability and predictability, with a consistent interest rate throughout the life of the loan. On the other hand, an adjustable-rate mortgage, as the name implies, can fluctuate over time, potentially leading to lower initial payments but increased risk down the road.

Loan Terms and Repayment Options

Beyond interest rates, you'll also need to consider the terms of your loan and your repayment options. The term of your loan, typically expressed in years (e.g., 15, 20, or 30), will determine the duration of your mortgage and the timeline for repayment. Additionally, you'll need to decide between conventional loans, FHA loans, VA loans, and other specialized products, each with its own set of pros and cons.

Down Payments and Closing Costs

But wait, there's more! Before you can close the deal on your dream home, you'll need to navigate the murky waters of down payments and closing costs. These upfront expenses can add up quickly, so it's essential to budget accordingly and explore potential assistance programs or down payment assistance grants that may be available to you.

The Path Ahead

As we wrap up our exploration of the home loan journey, remember that knowledge is power. By understanding the ins and outs of the mortgage process, you'll be better equipped to navigate the challenges ahead and emerge triumphant on the other side. So buckle up, dear reader, for the road ahead may be long and winding, but with determination and perseverance, we'll reach our destination together - the threshold of your dream home, keys in hand, heart brimming with excitement.

CHAPTER 2

The Importance of Paying Off Your Home Loan Early

Hey there, fellow dreamer of financial independence! Picture this: you've finally found your dream home, signed the dotted line, and now you're comfortably settled in. But there's a lingering thought gnawing at the back of your mind—your mortgage. It's that hefty loan hanging over your head, silently whispering reminders of interest rates and monthly payments.

Now, pause for a moment and imagine a life where you're not tethered to that mortgage. A life where the weight of debt doesn't overshadow your financial decisions. Intrigued? Well, my friend, that's the beauty of paying off your home loan early—a journey towards financial liberation and peace of mind.

Let's dive into the captivating world of why it's so crucial to bid farewell to that mortgage sooner rather than later.

1. Crushing the Interest Dragon

Ah, interest rates—the bane of every borrower's existence. They lurk in the shadows, quietly accumulating, and before you know it, you've paid a small fortune in interest alone. But fear not! Paying off your mortgage early is like slaying the interest dragon.

Think about it this way: the longer you take to pay off your loan, the more interest accrues. By accelerating your payments, you're essentially slashing through that interest monster, saving yourself a considerable sum in the long haul. It's not just about saving money; it's about regaining control over your finances and redirecting those funds towards your dreams.

2. Embracing Financial Freedom

Close your eyes and envision a life free from debt—no more monthly mortgage payments weighing you down. Paying off your home loan early opens the door to unparalleled financial freedom. Suddenly, your paycheck isn't stretched thin by looming obligations. Instead, you have the flexibility to invest in your passions, travel the world, or simply enjoy the peace of mind that comes with being debt-free.

Imagine the possibilities: starting that business you've always dreamed of, pursuing further education, or even retiring early without the burden of a mortgage hanging over your head. It's not just about the numbers; it's about reclaiming your life and charting your own course towards prosperity.

3. Building Wealth and Security

Now, let's talk about building wealth—the cornerstone of a secure financial future. Paying off your home loan early isn't just about eliminating debt; it's about laying the foundation for long-term prosperity.

Consider this: every dollar you funnel towards your mortgage is an investment in your own financial security. By paying off your loan ahead of schedule, you're effectively reallocating those funds towards wealth-building endeavors. Whether it's investing in the stock market, funding your retirement accounts, or diversifying your assets, you're taking proactive steps towards a brighter financial future.

Moreover, owning your home outright provides a sense of security that transcends monetary value. In an uncertain world, having a roof over your head free from the threat of foreclosure is priceless. It's the peace of mind that comes with knowing that, no matter what curveballs life throws your way, you have a sanctuary to call your own.

4. Liberating Yourself from Stress

Let's face it—financial stress is a silent but formidable foe. It creeps into every aspect of our lives, casting a shadow over our happiness and well-being. But paying off your home loan early? That's like waving a magic wand and banishing stress to the abyss.

Picture waking up each morning without the weight of debt pressing down on your shoulders. No more sleepless nights fretting over mortgage payments or interest rates. Instead, you're free to focus on the things that truly matter—your family, your passions, and your own personal growth.

By liberating yourself from the shackles of debt, you're not just improving your financial health; you're enhancing your overall quality of life. It's a transformative journey towards greater happiness, fulfillment, and inner peace.

5. Setting an Inspiring Example

Last but not least, let's talk about the ripple effect of paying off your home loan early. As you embark on this journey towards financial freedom, you're not just changing your own life; you're setting an inspiring example for others to follow.

Imagine the impact of your story—the friends, family members, and loved ones inspired to take control of their own financial destinies. Your actions speak volumes, serving as a beacon of hope and empowerment in a world often overshadowed by debt and uncertainty.

By paying off your mortgage ahead of schedule, you're not just shaping your own future; you're paving the way for a brighter tomorrow for generations to come. It's a legacy of empowerment, resilience, and unwavering determination—a legacy that transcends mere dollars and cents.

In conclusion, my fellow dreamers, paying off your home loan early isn't just a financial strategy; it's a life-changing decision with far-reaching implications. It's about reclaiming control over your finances, embracing freedom and security, and inspiring others to follow in your footsteps.

So, what are you waiting for? It's time to embark on this remarkable journey towards financial liberation. With each payment, you're not just inching closer to owning your home outright; you're unlocking a world of endless possibilities and infinite potential.

Here's to a future free from debt, filled with abundance, prosperity, and the boundless joy of living life on your own terms. Cheers to the extraordinary adventure that awaits as you pave your own path towards financial freedom!

CHAPTER 3

Common Challenges and Misconceptions: Demystifying the Roadblocks to Home Loan Repayment

Hello, my fellow adventurers in the realm of homeownership! Today, we're going to embark on a journey deep into the heart of the challenges and misconceptions that often plague those seeking to pay off their home loans. Strap in, because we're about to tackle these obstacles head-on and emerge victorious on the other side.

The Myth of Unattainability

First things first, let's address the elephant in the room - the myth that paying off your home loan early is an unattainable feat reserved for the financial elite. This misconception couldn't be further from the truth! While it's true that the journey to mortgage freedom may be long and arduous, it's entirely within reach for anyone with the determination and discipline to see it through.

The Challenge of Affordability

One of the most common challenges aspiring homeowners face is the perceived lack of affordability. With housing prices on the rise and wages struggling to keep pace, many feel as though homeownership is nothing more than a distant dream. But fear not, for there are countless resources and strategies available to help make homeownership a reality, even on a modest income.

The Trap of Comparison

In today's hyper-connected world, it's all too easy to fall into the trap of comparison. We see friends, family members, and neighbors living in seemingly perfect homes, and we can't help but wonder why we haven't achieved the same level of success. But here's the truth - everyone's journey is unique, and comparing your progress to others' will only serve to undermine your own accomplishments.

The Illusion of Instant Gratification

In our fast-paced society, we've become conditioned to expect instant gratification in all aspects of life, including homeownership. But the reality is that paying off your home loan early requires patience, perseverance, and a long-term mindset. It's a marathon, not a sprint, and success often comes to those who are willing to put in the hard work and dedication required to achieve their goals.

The Fear of Sacrifice

Another common misconception is the belief that paying off your home loan early requires significant sacrifice and deprivation. While it's true that some level of sacrifice may be necessary, it's important to remember that the journey towards financial freedom is ultimately a journey towards greater abundance and fulfillment. By prioritizing your financial goals and making conscious choices about how you allocate your resources, you'll find that the rewards far outweigh any perceived sacrifices.

The Misconception of Complexity

Finally, let's debunk the myth that paying off your home loan early is an impossibly complex task. While it's true that the mortgage process can be daunting at first glance, with its myriad terms, calculations, and paperwork, it's entirely manageable with the right guidance and support. By breaking the process down into manageable steps and arming yourself with knowledge, you'll find that navigating the intricacies of home loan repayment is well within your grasp.

CHAPTER 4

Part I: Maximizing Income Streams - Unleashing the Power of Financial Freedom

Hey there, fellow dreamers and doers! Welcome to the first phase of our epic journey towards paying off that pesky home loan faster than you ever thought possible. Get ready to roll up your sleeves, because in this part, we're diving headfirst into the exhilarating world of maximizing income streams.

The Power of Multiple Streams of Income

Now, I know what you're thinking - "But isn't one job enough?" Well, my friend, while a single income stream may keep the lights on, multiple streams of income have the power to light up your entire financial landscape. Imagine waking up to not just one paycheck, but multiple streams of income flowing into your bank account like a majestic river of financial abundance. Sounds pretty sweet, doesn't it?

Exploring Opportunities Beyond the 9-to-5 Grind

But where do you find these magical income streams, you ask? Fear not, for the world is brimming with opportunities just waiting to be seized. From freelancing and consulting gigs to rental properties and passive income streams, the possibilities are endless. So don't limit yourself to the confines of your nine-to-five job - venture out into the vast wilderness of opportunity and watch as your income potential soars to new heights.

The Side Hustle Revolution

Ah, the side hustle - the unsung hero of the modern era. In today's gig economy, the side hustle isn't just a way to make a few extra bucks - it's a full-blown revolution, a movement of everyday people taking control of their financial destinies and turning their passions into profits. So whether you're driving for rideshare companies, selling handmade crafts online, or monetizing your hobbies and interests in creative ways, there's a side hustle out there with your name on it.

Balancing Hustle with Heart

Of course, while the allure of multiple income streams may be tempting, it's essential to strike a balance between hustle and heart. After all, what good is financial freedom if you're burnt out, stressed out, and missing out on life's precious moments? So as you embark on your journey towards maximizing income streams, don't forget to prioritize self-care, nurture your relationships, and carve out time for the things that truly matter.

Dreaming Big and Scaling Up

But here's the thing - why stop at just a few extra bucks here and there when you could be building an empire? That's right, my friend - it's time to dream big and scale up your side hustles to new heights of success. What starts as a humble side gig has the potential to blossom into a thriving business empire, generating substantial income and opening up new opportunities for growth and expansion. So don't be afraid to think big, take calculated risks, and seize opportunities as they arise. The sky's the limit when it comes to maximizing income streams and unlocking the door to financial freedom.

CHAPTER 5

Exploring Additional Sources of Income: Unleashing Your Potential for Financial Growth

Hey there, fellow dreamers and doers! Are you ready to unlock the secrets to financial freedom and take control of your destiny? Well, you've come to the right place because in this section, we're diving deep into the exciting world of exploring additional sources of income. Get ready to discover new opportunities, unleash your creativity, and pave the way towards a brighter, more prosperous future.

Assessing Your Skills and Resources

First things first, let's take a moment to assess your skills and resources. What are you passionate about? What are you good at? What resources do you have at your disposal? Whether it's your expertise in a particular field, your knack for creativity, or your access to valuable resources, there's something unique about you that can be leveraged to generate additional income.

So take some time to reflect on your strengths, passions, and resources. Maybe you're a whiz at graphic design, a masterful wordsmith, or a DIY aficionado with a knack for crafting. Whatever it is, embrace it, own it, and use it to your advantage as you explore new avenues for generating income.

Freelancing and Consulting Opportunities

Next up, let's talk about freelancing and consulting opportunities. In today's digital age, the world is your oyster when it comes to freelancing and consulting gigs. Whether you're a seasoned professional with years of experience under your belt or a recent graduate just starting out, there are countless opportunities waiting to be seized.

From writing and editing to graphic design, web development, and beyond, there's a vast array of freelance opportunities available across a wide range of industries. And the best part? You have the freedom to choose projects that align with your skills, interests, and schedule, giving you unparalleled flexibility and control over your work-life balance.

So don't be afraid to put yourself out there, network like crazy, and showcase your skills and expertise to the world. With determination and perseverance, you'll soon find yourself landing lucrative freelance gigs and consulting opportunities that not only pad your bank account but also provide valuable experience and opportunities for growth.

Rental Income and Property Investments

Now let's turn our attention to rental income and property investments. Investing in real estate has long been touted as one of the most reliable ways to generate passive income and build wealth over time. Whether you're dipping your toes into the world of rental properties or diving headfirst into the realm of real estate investing, there are countless opportunities waiting to be seized.

From single-family homes and multi-unit properties to commercial real estate and vacation rentals, the possibilities are endless when it comes to generating rental income. And with the rise of platforms like Airbnb and VRBO, it's easier than ever to market your properties to a global audience and maximize your earning potential.

But investing in real estate isn't just about passive income - it's also about long-term wealth building and financial security. By leveraging the power of leverage, appreciation, and tax benefits, you can build a diversified real estate portfolio that generates steady income and grows in value over time, providing a solid foundation for your financial future.

Passive Income Streams

Last but certainly not least, let's talk about passive income streams. Passive income is the holy grail of financial independence - income that you earn with minimal effort or ongoing maintenance. From rental properties and dividend-paying stocks to royalties, licensing fees, and affiliate marketing, there are countless ways to generate passive income and build wealth over time.

But here's the thing about passive income - it's not truly passive in the beginning. It requires upfront effort, investment, and time to set up and scale. But once you've built a solid foundation, passive income streams have the potential to generate income indefinitely with minimal ongoing effort on your part.

So whether you're exploring rental properties, dividend-paying stocks, or digital products and courses, don't underestimate the power of passive income in your quest for financial freedom. With patience, persistence, and a willingness to invest in yourself and your future, you'll soon find yourself reaping the rewards of passive income and paving the way towards a brighter, more prosperous future.

CHAPTER 6

Leveraging Side Hustles for Financial Growth: Empowering Your Journey to Success

Hey there, fellow dreamers and doers! Are you ready to unlock the secrets to financial growth and take control of your destiny? Well, you've come to the right place because in this section, we're diving deep into the exhilarating world of leveraging side hustles to supercharge your income, achieve your financial goals, and live life on your own terms. So grab your favorite beverage, get cozy, and let's dive in!

Unleashing Your Potential

First things first, let's talk about unleashing your potential through side hustles. You see, side hustles aren't just about making a few extra bucks on the side - they're about tapping into your unique talents, passions, and interests to create additional streams of income that can transform your financial future. Whether you're a budding entrepreneur with big dreams or a seasoned professional looking to diversify your income, side hustles have the power to unlock your full potential and propel you towards success.

Identifying Profitable Side Hustle Ideas

Now, let's talk about identifying profitable side hustle ideas. With so many opportunities out there, it can be overwhelming to know where to start. But fear not, because I'm here to help you uncover hidden gems and discover side hustles that not only align with your skills and interests but also have the potential to generate substantial income.

From freelancing in your area of expertise to launching an e-commerce store, monetizing your hobbies and passions, or even starting a blog or YouTube channel, the possibilities are endless when it comes to side hustle ideas. So take some time to explore your options, brainstorm ideas, and think outside the box. Who knows? You might just stumble upon the perfect side hustle that not only pads your bank account but also brings you joy and fulfillment.

Balancing Work and Personal Life

Of course, while the allure of side hustles may be tempting, it's essential to strike a balance between work and personal life. After all, what good is financial success if you're burnt out, stressed out, and missing out on life's precious moments?

So as you embark on your side hustle journey, remember to prioritize self-care, nurture your relationships, and carve out time for the things that truly matter. Whether it's spending quality time with loved ones, pursuing hobbies and interests, or simply taking a moment to relax and recharge, don't underestimate the importance of maintaining a healthy work-life balance.

Scaling Up for Increased Earnings

But here's the thing - why stop at just a few extra bucks here and there when you could be scaling up your side hustles for increased earnings? That's right, my friend - it's time to dream big and take your side hustles to the next level.

Whether it's expanding your client base, diversifying your product offerings, investing in marketing and promotion, or even hiring help to free up your time, there are countless ways to scale up your side hustles and increase your earning potential. So don't be afraid to think outside the box, take calculated risks, and seize opportunities as they arise.

And remember, scaling up your side hustles isn't just about making more money - it's also about creating more freedom and flexibility in your life. By increasing your income streams and diversifying your sources of revenue, you'll have the power to take control of your financial destiny and live life on your own terms.

Conclusion: Your Journey Begins Here

As we bring our exploration of leveraging side hustles for financial growth to a close, I hope you feel inspired and empowered to take control of your financial destiny. Whether you're identifying profitable side hustle ideas, balancing work and personal life, or scaling up your side hustles for increased earnings, the opportunities are endless when it comes to achieving financial success.

So go forth, dear dreamer, and unleash the power of side hustles. Your journey towards financial freedom begins here, and I have every confidence that you'll soon find yourself on the path to a brighter, more prosperous future.

CHAPTER 7

Part II: Budgeting and Financial Management

Mastering Your Money: The Ultimate Guide to Budgeting and Financial Management

Hey there, fellow financial adventurer! Ready to embark on a journey towards mastering your money and taking control of your financial destiny? Well, buckle up because we're about to dive headfirst into the exhilarating world of budgeting and financial management.

1. Unveiling the Power of Budgeting

Let's kick things off by demystifying the age-old concept of budgeting. Think of your budget as a roadmap for your financial journey—a strategic plan that guides your spending, saving, and investing decisions.

But here's the thing: budgeting isn't about restriction or deprivation; it's about empowerment and freedom. By creating a budget, you're taking the reins of your financial future and steering it towards prosperity.

Imagine having a clear picture of where your money is going each month. No more guessing games or sleepless nights worrying about unexpected expenses. With a well-crafted budget, you're equipped with the knowledge and foresight to make informed financial choices that align with your goals and values.

2. The Art of Tracking Your Expenses

Now, let's talk about the cornerstone of effective budgeting: tracking your expenses. It's time to roll up your sleeves and get up close and personal with your spending habits.

Tracking your expenses isn't just about tallying up receipts and logging transactions; it's about gaining valuable insights into your financial behavior. It's about identifying patterns, pinpointing areas where you can cut back, and making conscious decisions about where to allocate your hard-earned dollars.

But fear not, my friend, for tracking your expenses doesn't have to be a tedious chore. Thanks to the wonders of modern technology, there are a plethora of user-friendly apps and tools available to streamline the process. From budgeting apps that categorize your expenses automatically to digital wallets that track your spending in real-time, the options are endless.

So, grab your smartphone and embark on this enlightening journey of self-discovery. You'll be amazed at how a little bit of mindfulness and intentionality can transform your financial outlook for the better.

3. Setting SMART Financial Goals

Now that you've mastered the art of budgeting and expense tracking, it's time to set your sights on the future. Cue the entrance of SMART financial goals—specific, measurable, achievable, relevant, and time-bound.

But what exactly constitutes a SMART financial goal, you ask? Well, let's break it down:

Specific: Your goal should be clear and concise, leaving no room for ambiguity. Instead of saying, "I want to save money," try, "I want to save $5,000 for a down payment on a new car."

Measurable: Your goal should be quantifiable so that you can track your progress along the way. Set concrete milestones and benchmarks to gauge your success.

Achievable: While it's important to dream big, it's equally crucial to set goals that are within reach. Be realistic about your financial situation and capabilities.

Relevant: Your goal should be aligned with your values, priorities, and long-term aspirations. Make sure it's something that truly matters to you.

Time-bound: Give yourself a deadline to work towards, creating a sense of urgency and accountability.

Whether your goals revolve around saving for a dream vacation, paying off debt, or building an emergency fund, the key is to approach them with intentionality and determination. With a clear roadmap in place, you'll be well on your way to turning your financial dreams into reality.

4. Embracing the Power of Saving and Investing

Ah, saving and investing—the dynamic duo of wealth-building. It's time to harness their combined power and supercharge your financial journey.

First up, let's talk about saving. Whether it's stashing away money for a rainy day or building a nest egg for retirement, saving is the foundation of financial security. But it's not just about socking away cash under your mattress; it's about making your money work for you.

Enter the world of investing. From stocks and bonds to real estate and mutual funds, there are endless avenues for growing your wealth and securing your financial future. But before you dive in headfirst, it's crucial to do your homework, assess your risk tolerance, and seek out professional guidance if needed.

Remember, investing is a long-term game, and patience is key. While the allure of quick riches may be tempting, it's the steady, disciplined approach that ultimately leads to success.

5. Navigating Financial Challenges with Resilience

No financial journey is without its fair share of bumps in the road. From unexpected expenses to economic downturns, life has a way of throwing us curveballs when we least expect it. But fear not, for with a solid foundation in budgeting and financial management, you possess the resilience and fortitude to weather any storm.

In times of hardship, don't be afraid to lean on your budget as a guiding light. Trim unnecessary expenses, explore alternative sources of income, and above all, remain adaptable and flexible in the face of adversity.

Remember, it's not about avoiding challenges altogether; it's about how you respond to them that truly matters. With a proactive mindset and a steadfast commitment to your financial goals, you'll emerge stronger and more resilient than ever before.

In conclusion, my fellow financial adventurers, mastering the art of budgeting and financial management isn't just about crunching numbers and balancing spreadsheets. It's about empowerment, freedom, and taking control of your financial destiny.

So, seize the reins, embark on this exhilarating journey, and unlock the boundless potential that awaits. With each step forward, you're not just inching closer to financial security; you're forging a path towards a future filled with abundance, prosperity, and unwavering peace of mind.

Here's to embracing the power of budgeting and financial management—together, we'll conquer mountains, defy odds, and chart a course towards financial freedom like never before. Cheers to your extraordinary adventure ahead!

CHAPTER 8

Fast Track to Mortgage Freedom: Crafting a Comprehensive Budget Plan

Hey there, fellow dreamer of homeownership and financial independence! Are you ready to embark on an exhilarating journey towards paying off your home loan faster than you ever thought possible? Well, hold onto your hats because we're about to dive deep into the captivating world of creating a comprehensive budget plan tailored specifically to accelerate your mortgage payoff.

1. The Power of Purposeful Planning

Let's kick things off by demystifying the art of budgeting. Picture your budget as a roadmap—a strategic blueprint that guides your financial decisions and propels you towards your goals. But not just any goals—we're talking about the ultimate goal: paying off your home loan ahead of schedule.

Creating a comprehensive budget plan isn't just about crunching numbers and cutting expenses; it's about intentionality and purposeful planning. It's about aligning every dollar you earn with your overarching objective of achieving mortgage freedom.

Imagine the satisfaction of watching your mortgage balance dwindle with each passing month, knowing that you're inching closer to owning your home outright. With a well-crafted budget plan as your compass, you'll navigate the twists and turns of your financial journey with confidence and clarity.

2. Embracing the Power of Prioritization

Now, let's talk about the power of prioritization. When it comes to paying off your home loan fast, every dollar counts. That means making tough choices and prioritizing your spending in alignment with your goals.

Take a close look at your expenses and identify areas where you can trim the fat. Do you really need that daily latte from the fancy coffee shop? Can you cut back on dining out and cook more meals at home? By scrutinizing your spending habits and distinguishing between needs and wants, you'll free up valuable resources to put towards your mortgage payoff.

But prioritization isn't just about cutting back on discretionary expenses—it's also about maximizing your income potential. Whether it's picking up a side hustle, negotiating a raise at work, or exploring passive income streams, every additional dollar you earn brings you one step closer to mortgage freedom.

3. Harnessing the Power of Automation

Now, let's talk about streamlining your budgeting process with the power of automation. In today's digital age, there are a plethora of tools and apps available to simplify and streamline your financial management.

From budgeting apps that categorize your expenses automatically to automatic bill pay services that ensure your bills are paid on time every month, automation is a game-changer when it comes to staying on track with your budget plan.

But automation isn't just about convenience—it's also about consistency. By setting up automated transfers to your mortgage account each month, you'll ensure that you're consistently chipping away at your loan balance without even lifting a finger.

4. Creating a Cushion with an Emergency Fund

Now, let's talk about the importance of creating a cushion with an emergency fund. Life has a way of throwing us curveballs when we least expect it, and having a financial safety net in place is crucial to weathering any storm.

While your primary focus may be on paying off your home loan, it's essential to set aside funds for unexpected expenses such as medical emergencies, car repairs, or job loss. By building an emergency fund, you'll avoid the need to dip into your mortgage payoff funds when life inevitably throws you a curveball.

But here's the key: your emergency fund should be separate from your mortgage payoff funds. Keep it in a high-yield savings account or money market fund where it's easily accessible in times of need, but separate enough that you're not tempted to dip into it for non-emergencies.

5. Celebrating Milestones and Staying Motivated

Last but not least, let's talk about celebrating milestones and staying motivated on your journey towards mortgage freedom. Paying off your home loan ahead of schedule is no small feat, and it's essential to acknowledge and celebrate your progress along the way.

Set mini-milestones and rewards for yourself as you reach certain benchmarks in your mortgage payoff journey. Whether it's treating yourself to a nice dinner out or splurging on a small indulgence, these rewards serve as powerful motivators to keep you focused and engaged.

But remember, paying off your home loan faster is a marathon, not a sprint. There will be ups and downs along the way, but with determination, discipline, and a comprehensive budget plan as your guide, you'll ultimately cross the finish line and achieve the ultimate victory of mortgage freedom.

In conclusion, my fellow dreamers of homeownership and financial independence, creating a comprehensive budget plan is the key to unlocking the fast track to paying off your home loan ahead of schedule. By harnessing the power of purposeful planning, prioritization, automation, emergency funds, and motivation, you'll chart a course towards mortgage freedom like never before.

So, what are you waiting for? It's time to roll up your sleeves, craft your budget plan, and embark on this exhilarating journey towards a future free from mortgage payments. With each dollar you save and every milestone you reach, you're one step closer to realizing your dreams of homeownership and financial security.

Here's to the extraordinary adventure that awaits as you pave your own path towards mortgage freedom! Cheers to you and your unwavering commitment to financial success!

CHAPTER 9

Turbocharge Your Mortgage Payoff: Mastering Expense and Income Tracking

Hey there, fellow financial trailblazers! Are you ready to unlock the secrets to paying off your home loan at warp speed? Well, buckle up because we're about to dive deep into the exhilarating world of tracking expenses and income—your ticket to turbocharging your mortgage payoff and achieving financial freedom faster than you ever thought possible.

1. Unveiling the Power of Tracking Expenses

Let's kick things off by shining a spotlight on the transformative power of tracking expenses. Picture your expenses as puzzle pieces scattered across the vast landscape of your financial journey. Without a clear understanding of where each piece fits, you're left with a fragmented picture of your financial reality.

But fear not, my friend, for tracking expenses is like wielding a magnifying glass, allowing you to zoom in on every detail of your spending habits. It's about shining a light on those seemingly insignificant purchases—the daily coffees, the impulse buys, the subscription services—that collectively chip away at your financial freedom.

By meticulously tracking your expenses, you'll gain invaluable insights into your spending patterns, identify areas where you can cut back, and reclaim control over your financial destiny. It's not just about crunching numbers; it's about empowerment and enlightenment—a journey towards financial clarity and liberation.

2. Embracing the Art of Income Tracking

Now, let's flip the script and shine a spotlight on the often-overlooked practice of income tracking. Your income is the lifeblood of your financial journey—the fuel that powers your aspirations and propels you towards your goals.

But here's the thing: not all income is created equal. From your regular paycheck to side hustles, passive income streams, and unexpected windfalls, each source of income plays a unique role in shaping your financial landscape.

By tracking your income with the same diligence and precision as your expenses, you'll gain a comprehensive understanding of your financial ecosystem. You'll identify opportunities to maximize your earning potential, leverage your skills and talents, and accelerate your journey towards mortgage freedom.

3. Creating a Budget with Purpose and Precision

Now that you've mastered the art of tracking expenses and income, it's time to weave these insights into the fabric of a comprehensive budget—one that serves as a roadmap to paying off your home loan fast.

But not just any budget will suffice. We're talking about a budget infused with purpose and precision—a strategic blueprint that aligns every dollar you earn with your overarching goal of mortgage freedom.

Start by categorizing your expenses into essential and discretionary categories. Essential expenses— think mortgage payments, utilities, groceries—are non-negotiables that keep the wheels of your financial life turning. Discretionary expenses, on the other hand, are areas where you have more flexibility to cut back and reallocate funds towards your mortgage payoff.

Next, factor in your income streams and allocate them towards your various expense categories. Be strategic in your approach, prioritizing your mortgage payoff goal and funneling as much income as possible towards accelerating your loan repayment.

4. Leveraging Technology to Simplify and Streamline

Now, let's talk about leveraging technology to simplify and streamline your expense and income tracking efforts. In today's digital age, there's a treasure trove of apps, tools, and software available to automate and optimize your financial management.

From budgeting apps that sync with your bank accounts and credit cards to expense tracking tools that categorize your spending automatically, the options are endless. Find the tools that resonate with your needs and preferences, and harness their power to take your financial management to the next level.

But remember, technology is a tool, not a solution in and of itself. While these apps and tools can certainly simplify the tracking process, it's crucial to remain actively engaged in managing your finances and making informed decisions based on the insights they provide.

5. Celebrating Victories and Staying Motivated

Last but certainly not least, let's talk about celebrating victories and staying motivated on your journey towards mortgage freedom. Paying off your home loan ahead of schedule is no small feat, and it's essential to acknowledge and celebrate your progress along the way.

Set mini-milestones and rewards for yourself as you reach certain benchmarks in your mortgage payoff journey. Whether it's treating yourself to a nice dinner out, splurging on a small indulgence, or simply taking a moment to reflect on how far you've come, these rewards serve as powerful motivators to keep you focused and engaged.

But remember, paying off your home loan faster is a marathon, not a sprint. There will be ups and downs along the way, but with determination, discipline, and a comprehensive expense and income tracking plan as your guide, you'll ultimately cross the finish line and achieve the ultimate victory of mortgage freedom.

In conclusion, my fellow financial trailblazers, tracking expenses and income isn't just about crunching numbers; it's about empowerment, enlightenment, and taking control of your financial destiny. By shining a light on your spending habits, maximizing your earning potential, and weaving these insights into a comprehensive budget plan, you'll pave the way towards mortgage freedom faster than you ever thought possible.

So, what are you waiting for? It's time to roll up your sleeves, harness the power of tracking expenses and income, and embark on this exhilarating journey towards a future free from mortgage payments. With each dollar you save and every milestone you reach, you're one step closer to realizing your dreams of homeownership and financial security.

72 | P a g e

Here's to the extraordinary adventure that awaits as you pave your own path towards mortgage freedom! Cheers to you and your unwavering commitment to financial success!

CHAPTER 10

Fast-Track Your Mortgage: Setting Realistic Financial Goals for Rapid Loan Repayment

Hey there, fellow financial champions! Are you ready to supercharge your journey towards paying off your home loan faster than you ever thought possible? Well, get ready to unleash the power of setting realistic financial goals, because we're about to embark on an electrifying adventure towards mortgage freedom!

1. The Power of Purposeful Planning

Let's kick things off by diving deep into the transformative power of setting realistic financial goals. Picture your goals as guiding stars—a constellation of aspirations that illuminate the path towards your ultimate destination: paying off your home loan ahead of schedule.

But here's the kicker: setting goals isn't just about wishful thinking or shooting for the stars; it's about purposeful planning and deliberate action. It's about breaking down your big, audacious goal of mortgage freedom into manageable, bite-sized chunks that you can tackle one step at a time.

By setting realistic financial goals, you're not just dreaming—you're strategizing, plotting, and scheming your way towards success. It's the difference between wandering aimlessly through the wilderness and charting a course towards your desired destination with confidence and clarity.

2. The Art of SMART Goal Setting

Now, let's talk about the art of SMART goal setting—a tried-and-true framework for crafting goals that are Specific, Measurable, Achievable, Relevant, and Time-bound.

Specific: Your goal should be clear and concise, leaving no room for ambiguity. Instead of saying, "I want to pay off my home loan faster," try, "I want to pay an extra $500 towards my mortgage each month."

Measurable: Your goal should be quantifiable so that you can track your progress along the way. Set concrete milestones and benchmarks to gauge your success.

Achievable: While it's important to dream big, it's equally crucial to set goals that are within reach. Be realistic about your financial situation and capabilities.

Relevant: Your goal should be aligned with your values, priorities, and long-term aspirations. Make sure it's something that truly matters to you.

Time-bound: Give yourself a deadline to work towards, creating a sense of urgency and accountability.

By applying the SMART criteria to your financial goals, you're setting yourself up for success and ensuring that you have a clear roadmap to follow on your journey towards mortgage freedom.

3. Prioritizing Mortgage Payoff in Your Financial Goals

Now that we've established the importance of setting SMART goals, let's talk about prioritizing mortgage payoff in your financial goals lineup. Your home loan is likely one of your most significant financial obligations, and paying it off ahead of schedule can free up valuable resources for other goals and aspirations.

Start by evaluating your current financial situation and determining how much extra you can realistically afford to put towards your mortgage each month. Then, incorporate this additional payment into your budget as a non-negotiable expense, treating it with the same level of importance as your other financial obligations.

But here's the beauty of prioritizing mortgage payoff in your financial goals: with each extra payment you make, you're not just reducing your loan balance—you're also saving yourself thousands of dollars in interest over the life of the loan. It's a win-win scenario that puts you one step closer to mortgage freedom with every dollar you save.

4. Breaking Down Your Mortgage Payoff Goal

Now that you've prioritized mortgage payoff in your financial goals lineup, it's time to break down your big, audacious goal into smaller, more manageable milestones. Instead of fixating on the daunting prospect of paying off your entire home loan at once, focus on making steady progress towards your goal one step at a time.

Start by setting monthly or quarterly targets for additional mortgage payments, gradually increasing the amount as your financial situation allows. Celebrate each milestone along the way, whether it's paying off a certain percentage of your loan or reaching a specific dollar amount in extra payments.

But remember, progress is progress, no matter how small. By breaking down your mortgage payoff goal into bite-sized chunks, you'll stay motivated and inspired as you inch closer to the finish line with each passing milestone.

5. Staying Flexible and Adaptable

Last but not least, let's talk about the importance of staying flexible and adaptable in your pursuit of mortgage freedom. Life has a way of throwing us curveballs when we least expect it, and it's essential to roll with the punches and adjust your goals and plans accordingly.

If unexpected expenses arise or your financial situation changes, don't be afraid to reassess your goals and make adjustments as needed. Maybe you need to scale back on your extra mortgage payments temporarily or explore alternative income streams to stay on track. Whatever the case may be, remember that flexibility is the key to long-term success.

In conclusion, my fellow financial champions, setting realistic financial goals is the secret sauce to paying off your home loan faster than you ever thought possible. By applying the SMART criteria, prioritizing mortgage payoff, breaking down your goal into manageable milestones, and staying flexible and adaptable along the way, you'll chart a course towards mortgage freedom with confidence and clarity.

So, what are you waiting for? It's time to roll up your sleeves, unleash the power of setting realistic financial goals, and embark on this electrifying adventure towards a future free from mortgage payments. With each milestone you reach and every dollar you save, you're one step closer to realizing your dreams of homeownership and financial security.

Here's to the extraordinary journey that awaits as you pave your own path towards mortgage freedom! Cheers to you and your unwavering commitment to financial success!

CHAPTER 11

Accelerate Your Mortgage Payoff: The Power of Prioritizing Debt Repayment

Hey there, fellow financial warriors! Are you ready to unleash the secret weapon in your arsenal for paying off your home loan at lightning speed? Get ready to dive deep into the exhilarating world of prioritizing debt repayment—the ultimate strategy for turbocharging your journey towards mortgage freedom!

1. Understanding the Weight of Debt

Let's kick things off by shining a spotlight on the elephant in the room: debt. Whether it's credit card balances, student loans, or, most notably, your home loan, debt can feel like a heavy burden weighing you down and holding you back from achieving your financial dreams.

But here's the thing: debt doesn't have to be a life sentence. By taking proactive steps to prioritize debt repayment, you can break free from its grasp and reclaim control over your financial future. It's not just about chipping away at your loan balance—it's about liberating yourself from the shackles of debt and paving the way towards a brighter tomorrow.

2. The Power of Prioritization

Now, let's talk about the transformative power of prioritization. When it comes to paying off your home loan fast, every dollar counts. That means making tough choices and focusing your financial resources on the debts that matter most.

Start by taking stock of your outstanding debts and identifying which ones carry the highest interest rates. These are your financial foes—the ones that are costing you the most money in interest charges each month.

Next, prioritize your debt repayment efforts by tackling these high-interest debts first. By focusing your financial resources on paying off these debts as quickly as possible, you'll minimize the amount of interest you pay over time and free up more money to put towards your mortgage payoff.

3. The Avalanche vs. Snowball Method

When it comes to prioritizing debt repayment, there are two popular strategies to choose from: the avalanche method and the snowball method. Let's take a closer look at each:

Avalanche Method: With the avalanche method, you prioritize your debts based on their interest rates, starting with the debt carrying the highest interest rate and working your way down to the lowest. This approach allows you to minimize the total amount of interest you pay over time and pay off your debts more efficiently.

Snowball Method: With the snowball method, you prioritize your debts based on their balances, starting with the smallest debt and working your way up to the largest. While this approach may not save you as much money in interest as the avalanche method, it can be psychologically motivating to see smaller debts eliminated quickly, providing a sense of momentum and progress.

Ultimately, the choice between the avalanche and snowball methods comes down to personal preference and what works best for your financial situation. Whether you prefer to focus on minimizing interest costs or gaining momentum through quick wins, both strategies can be effective in helping you achieve your goal of paying off your home loan fast.

4. Cutting Back and Increasing Cash Flow

Now, let's talk about freeing up extra cash to put towards your debt repayment efforts. One of the most effective ways to accelerate your mortgage payoff is to cut back on non-essential expenses and increase your cash flow.

Start by taking a close look at your monthly budget and identifying areas where you can trim the fat. Do you really need that daily latte from the fancy coffee shop, or could you brew your own at home for a fraction of the cost? Can you cut back on dining out and cook more meals at home? By scrutinizing your spending habits and distinguishing between needs and wants, you'll free up valuable resources to put towards your debt repayment goals.

But cutting back on expenses is just one piece of the puzzle. You can also explore opportunities to increase your income, whether it's picking up a side hustle, negotiating a raise at work, or monetizing a hobby or skill. Every additional dollar you earn brings you one step closer to mortgage freedom and accelerates your journey towards financial independence.

5. Celebrating Victories and Staying Motivated

Last but certainly not least, let's talk about celebrating victories and staying motivated on your journey towards mortgage freedom. Paying off your home loan ahead of schedule is no small feat, and it's essential to acknowledge and celebrate your progress along the way.

Set mini-milestones and rewards for yourself as you reach certain benchmarks in your debt repayment journey. Whether it's paying off a certain percentage of your total debt or eliminating a specific high-interest account, these rewards serve as powerful motivators to keep you focused and engaged.

But remember, paying off your home loan faster is a marathon, not a sprint. There will be ups and downs along the way, but with determination, discipline, and a laser-like focus on prioritizing debt repayment, you'll ultimately cross the finish line and achieve the ultimate victory of mortgage freedom.

In conclusion, my fellow financial warriors, prioritizing debt repayment is the secret weapon in your arsenal for paying off your home loan fast. By focusing your financial resources on high-interest debts, leveraging the avalanche or snowball method, cutting back on expenses, increasing your income, and staying motivated along the way, you'll accelerate your journey towards mortgage freedom and unlock a world of endless possibilities.

So, what are you waiting for? It's time to roll up your sleeves, unleash the power of prioritization, and embark on this exhilarating adventure towards a future free from mortgage payments. With each debt you pay off and every milestone you reach, you're one step closer to realizing your dreams of homeownership and financial security.

Here's to the extraordinary journey that awaits as you pave your own path towards mortgage freedom! Cheers to you and your unwavering commitment to financial success!

CHAPTER 12

Slash Your Expenses, Supercharge Your Savings: The Ultimate Guide to Paying Off Your Home Loan Fast

Hey there, financial trailblazers! Are you ready to kick your mortgage repayment into high gear and sprint towards homeownership freedom? Well, buckle up because we're about to embark on an exhilarating journey filled with savvy tips and tricks to trim expenses, boost savings, and pay off your home loan faster than you ever thought possible!

1. The Power of Penny Pinching

Let's kick things off by diving deep into the transformative power of trimming expenses. Picture your budget as a garden—lush, green, and brimming with potential. But amidst the blooms, there are weeds lurking—unnecessary expenses that choke your financial growth and hinder your progress towards mortgage freedom.

But fear not, my friend, for with a little bit of savvy and ingenuity, you can prune away those financial weeds and cultivate a budget that thrives. Start by taking a close look at your monthly expenses and identifying areas where you can cut back without sacrificing your quality of life.

Maybe it's dining out less often and cooking more meals at home, or canceling that gym membership you never use. Perhaps it's negotiating lower rates on your bills, like cable, internet, or insurance. By scrutinizing your spending habits and distinguishing between needs and wants, you'll uncover hidden opportunities to trim expenses and redirect those savings towards your home loan repayment.

2. Harnessing the Power of Budgeting

Now that we've identified areas to trim expenses, let's talk about the cornerstone of effective financial management: budgeting. Think of your budget as a roadmap—a strategic plan that guides your spending, saving, and investing decisions.

But here's the thing: budgeting isn't about restriction or deprivation; it's about empowerment and freedom. By creating a budget, you're taking control of your financial destiny and directing your resources towards your goals—like paying off your home loan ahead of schedule.

Start by outlining your income and fixed expenses, like mortgage payments, utilities, and groceries. Then, allocate a portion of your income towards discretionary expenses, like dining out, entertainment, and shopping. The key is to strike a balance that allows you to enjoy life while still making progress towards your financial goals.

But don't stop there—track your spending regularly and adjust your budget as needed to stay on track. Whether you use a spreadsheet, an app, or good old-fashioned pen and paper, the important thing is to be mindful of your spending and make intentional choices that align with your priorities.

3. Embracing the Art of Frugal Living

Now, let's talk about embracing the art of frugal living—a lifestyle that prioritizes value over extravagance and mindfulness over mindless consumption. Frugality isn't about deprivation or sacrifice; it's about making deliberate choices that maximize your happiness and financial well-being.

Start by reevaluating your spending habits and challenging yourself to find creative ways to save money. Maybe it's shopping for groceries at discount stores or buying generic brands instead of name brands. Perhaps it's cutting back on impulse purchases and embracing a "wait 24 hours" rule before making non-essential purchases.

But frugality isn't just about cutting back—it's also about finding joy and fulfillment in simple pleasures. Whether it's hosting a potluck dinner with friends instead of going out to an expensive restaurant or enjoying a movie night at home instead of hitting the theater, there are countless ways to live well on a budget.

4. Maximizing Your Savings Potential

Now that we've trimmed expenses and embraced frugality, let's talk about maximizing your savings potential. Saving money isn't just about cutting back on spending—it's also about making the most of every dollar you earn.

Start by automating your savings and setting up automatic transfers from your checking account to your savings or investment accounts. Treat your savings like a non-negotiable expense, just like your mortgage payment or utility bill, and prioritize it accordingly.

Next, take advantage of high-yield savings accounts, certificates of deposit (CDs), or other low-risk investment options to grow your savings over time. While the returns may not be as high as riskier investments, these vehicles offer stability and security, making them ideal for short-term goals like paying off your home loan.

But don't stop there—look for opportunities to increase your income and boost your savings rate even further. Whether it's picking up a side hustle, freelancing in your spare time, or monetizing a hobby or skill, every additional dollar you earn brings you one step closer to mortgage freedom.

5. Celebrating Milestones and Staying Motivated

Last but certainly not least, let's talk about celebrating milestones and staying motivated on your journey towards mortgage freedom. Paying off your home loan ahead of schedule is no small feat, and it's essential to acknowledge and celebrate your progress along the way.

Set mini-milestones and rewards for yourself as you reach certain benchmarks in your home loan repayment journey. Whether it's paying off a certain percentage of your loan balance or reaching a specific dollar amount in extra payments, these rewards serve as powerful motivators to keep you focused and engaged.

But remember, paying off your home loan faster is a marathon, not a sprint. There will be ups and downs along the way, but with determination, discipline, and a commitment to trimming expenses and increasing savings, you'll ultimately cross the finish line and achieve the ultimate victory of mortgage freedom.

Therefore my fellow financial warriors, trimming expenses and increasing savings is the secret sauce to paying off your home loan fast. By embracing frugality, maximizing your savings potential, and staying focused on your goals, you'll accelerate your journey towards mortgage freedom and unlock a world of endless possibilities.

So, what are you waiting for? It's time to roll up your sleeves, slash those expenses, and supercharge your savings. With each dollar you save and every milestone you reach, you're one step closer to realizing your dreams of homeownership and financial security.

Here's to the extraordinary journey that awaits as you pave your own path towards mortgage freedom! Cheers to you and your unwavering commitment to financial success!

CHAPTER 13

Slash, Save, Succeed: The Art of Analyzing and Cutting Unnecessary Expenses to Accelerate Your Home Loan Repayment

Hey there, financial superheroes! Are you ready to unlock the secrets to paying off your home loan faster than you ever thought possible? Well, get ready to dive deep into the thrilling world of analyzing and cutting unnecessary expenses—a surefire strategy for turbocharging your journey towards mortgage freedom and achieving your financial dreams!

1. The Hidden Impact of Unnecessary Expenses

Let's kick things off by shining a spotlight on the sneaky culprits that lurk in the shadows of your budget: unnecessary expenses. These are the silent saboteurs that chip away at your financial progress, diverting precious resources away from your goal of paying off your home loan ahead of schedule.

But fear not, my friend, for with a keen eye and a little detective work, you can uncover these hidden villains and banish them from your budget once and for all. It's time to take a closer look at your spending habits and identify areas where you can trim the fat and redirect those savings towards your mortgage repayment.

2. The Power of Intentional Spending

Now, let's talk about the transformative power of intentional spending. Picture your budget as a canvas—a blank slate waiting to be painted with purpose and intentionality. By taking control of your spending and making deliberate choices that align with your goals, you can wield your financial resources like a master artist, creating a masterpiece of financial success and security.

Start by auditing your expenses and identifying recurring payments that may no longer serve you. Do you really need that subscription service you rarely use, or could you put that money towards your mortgage instead? Are you overspending on dining out or entertainment, when a home-cooked meal or a movie night in could be just as enjoyable?

By scrutinizing your spending habits and distinguishing between needs and wants, you'll uncover opportunities to cut unnecessary expenses and reclaim control over your financial destiny. It's not about deprivation or sacrifice—it's about prioritizing what truly matters and channeling your resources towards your goals.

3. Identifying Problem Areas

Now that we've established the importance of intentional spending, let's talk about identifying problem areas in your budget. These are the areas where your spending tends to spiral out of control, diverting valuable resources away from your goal of paying off your home loan faster.

Start by taking a close look at your discretionary expenses—the non-essential purchases that can add up quickly if left unchecked. This could include dining out, entertainment, shopping, or any other indulgences that may be draining your bank account.

Next, examine your fixed expenses—things like utilities, insurance, and subscriptions—to see if there are any opportunities to reduce or eliminate unnecessary costs. Can you renegotiate your cable or internet bill for a lower rate, or switch to a more affordable insurance provider? Every dollar you save on fixed expenses is another dollar you can put towards your mortgage repayment.

4. Strategies for Cutting Expenses

Now that we've identified problem areas in your budget, let's talk about strategies for cutting expenses and maximizing your savings potential. There are countless ways to trim the fat and free up extra cash to put towards your home loan repayment—here are just a few ideas to get you started:

Cut back on dining out and entertainment by cooking more meals at home and exploring free or low-cost activities in your area.

Cancel or downgrade subscription services you don't use frequently, like streaming platforms, gym memberships, or magazine subscriptions.

Shop smarter by comparing prices, using coupons or discount codes, and avoiding impulse purchases.

Reduce energy usage and utility costs by turning off lights and appliances when not in use, sealing drafts, and investing in energy-efficient upgrades.

Refinance high-interest debt or consolidate multiple debts into a single, lower-interest loan to reduce interest costs and streamline your repayment process.

5. The Power of Tracking and Accountability

Last but certainly not least, let's talk about the power of tracking and accountability in your quest to cut unnecessary expenses and accelerate your home loan repayment. Keeping a close eye on your spending habits and holding yourself accountable for your financial choices are key components of success.

Start by tracking your expenses regularly, whether it's through a budgeting app, spreadsheet, or good old-fashioned pen and paper. Review your spending each month to identify areas where you can make improvements and adjust your budget accordingly.

But don't stop there—enlist the support of a friend, family member, or accountability partner to help you stay on track and keep you motivated. Share your goals and progress with them regularly, and celebrate your successes together as you work towards paying off your home loan faster.

So superheroes, analyzing and cutting unnecessary expenses is the secret weapon in your arsenal for paying off your home loan fast. By adopting a mindset of intentional spending, identifying problem areas in your budget, implementing strategies to trim the fat, and tracking your progress along the way, you'll accelerate your journey towards mortgage freedom and unlock a world of endless possibilities.

So, what are you waiting for? It's time to roll up your sleeves, unleash the power of intentional spending, and slash those unnecessary expenses.

With each dollar you save and every expense you cut, you're one step closer to realizing your dreams of homeownership and financial security.

CHAPTER 14

Mastering the Art of Negotiation: How to Score Better Deals and Discounts to Accelerate Your Home Loan Payoff

Hey there, savvy negotiators! Are you ready to unlock the secrets to slashing expenses, maximizing savings, and turbocharging your journey towards paying off your home loan faster than you ever thought possible? Well, get ready to dive deep into the exhilarating world of negotiation—the ultimate weapon in your arsenal for achieving financial freedom and homeownership success!

1. The Power of Negotiation

Let's kick things off by shining a spotlight on the transformative power of negotiation. Negotiation isn't just about haggling over prices or wrangling deals—it's about advocating for your financial well-being and maximizing the value of every dollar you spend.

Whether you're negotiating with a vendor, service provider, or even your employer, mastering the art of negotiation empowers you to secure better deals, lower rates, and higher savings—all of which can be channeled towards your goal of paying off your home loan faster.

2. Identifying Negotiation Opportunities

Now that we've established the importance of negotiation, let's talk about identifying opportunities to flex your negotiating muscles and score better deals and discounts. Negotiation opportunities abound in virtually every aspect of your financial life—from everyday purchases to major expenses.

Start by taking a close look at your monthly expenses and pinpointing areas where you can potentially negotiate better terms or lower rates.

This could include everything from your cable or internet bill to your insurance premiums, utilities, or even your mortgage interest rate.

Next, consider opportunities to negotiate better deals on big-ticket purchases, like furniture, appliances, or home renovations. Don't be afraid to shop around, compare prices, and leverage competing offers to negotiate the best possible deal.

3. Strategies for Successful Negotiation

Now that we've identified negotiation opportunities, let's talk about strategies for successful negotiation. Negotiation is as much an art as it is a science, requiring a combination of preparation, communication skills, and strategic thinking to achieve optimal outcomes.

Start by doing your homework and researching market prices, competitor offers, and industry standards before entering into negotiations. Knowledge is power, and being armed with information gives you a significant advantage at the bargaining table.

Next, approach negotiations with confidence and assertiveness, but also with a spirit of collaboration and mutual respect. Listen actively, ask questions, and seek to understand the other party's needs and constraints, as this can help you identify potential areas of compromise and find mutually beneficial solutions.

Be prepared to make concessions, but also know your limits and stick to your bottom line. Don't be afraid to walk away from a negotiation if the terms aren't favorable or if you're unable to reach a satisfactory agreement.

4. Negotiating Better Rates and Terms

Now that we've covered negotiation strategies, let's talk about specific tactics for negotiating better rates and terms on your expenses and purchases. Whether you're negotiating with service providers, vendors, or lenders, there are several key tactics you can employ to maximize your savings potential:

Comparison shopping: Gather competing offers and quotes from multiple providers and use them as leverage to negotiate better rates or discounts.

Loyalty discounts: Highlight your loyalty as a customer and inquire about loyalty discounts or special offers available to long-term customers.

Bundle discounts: Explore opportunities to bundle multiple services or products together to qualify for discounted rates or package deals.

Referral bonuses: Take advantage of referral programs or incentives offered by service providers to earn discounts or credits for referring new customers.

Promotional offers: Keep an eye out for promotional offers, seasonal sales, or limited-time discounts and take advantage of them to score better deals.

5. Negotiating Your Mortgage Interest Rate

Last but certainly not least, let's talk about negotiating your mortgage interest rate—the holy grail of negotiation opportunities when it comes to paying off your home loan faster. Your mortgage interest rate plays a significant role in determining the total cost of your loan and the amount of interest you'll pay over time, so negotiating a lower rate can translate into significant savings.

Start by shopping around and comparing offers from multiple lenders to get a sense of current market rates and terms. Armed with this information, approach your lender and inquire about their willingness to negotiate on your interest rate.

Highlight your strong credit history, stable income, and financial responsibility as reasons why you deserve a lower rate. Consider enlisting the help of a mortgage broker or loan officer to advocate on your behalf and negotiate the best possible terms.

Be prepared to negotiate other aspects of your mortgage as well, such as closing costs, loan origination fees, or prepayment penalties. Every dollar you save on these expenses is another dollar you can put towards your mortgage repayment and accelerate your journey towards homeownership freedom.

So mastering the art of negotiation is the ultimate weapon in your arsenal for paying off your home loan fast. By identifying negotiation opportunities, employing effective negotiation strategies, and advocating for better rates and terms, you'll maximize your savings potential and supercharge your journey towards financial freedom and homeownership success.

So, what are you waiting for? It's time to roll up your sleeves, unleash the power of negotiation, and score better deals and discounts on your expenses and purchases. With each negotiation victory, you're one step closer to realizing your dreams of paying off your home loan faster and achieving the ultimate victory of homeownership freedom.

Here's to the extraordinary journey that awaits as you pave your own path towards financial success! Cheers to you and your unwavering commitment to negotiation mastery!

CHAPTER 15

The Power of Preparedness: Building Emergency and Savings Funds to Accelerate Your Home Loan Repayment

Hey there, financial champions! Are you ready to fortify your financial fortress, protect yourself from unexpected curveballs, and supercharge your journey towards paying off your home loan faster than you ever thought possible? Well, get ready to dive deep into the exhilarating world of building emergency and savings funds—the ultimate strategy for achieving financial resilience and homeownership success!

1. The Importance of Financial Safety Nets

Let's kick things off by shining a spotlight on the importance of financial safety nets. Life is full of surprises, and having a robust emergency fund is like having a safety net to catch you when you fall. Whether it's a sudden medical expense, car repair, or unexpected job loss, having cash reserves set aside can provide peace of mind and protect you from financial disaster.

But here's the thing: building emergency and savings funds isn't just about protecting yourself from the unexpected—it's also about setting yourself up for success and achieving your long-term financial goals, like paying off your home loan ahead of schedule.

2. The Two Types of Financial Safety Nets

Now that we've established the importance of financial safety nets, let's talk about the two primary types: emergency funds and savings funds. While they serve similar purposes—to provide financial security and flexibility—they each have distinct purposes and characteristics.

Emergency Fund: Think of your emergency fund as your first line of defense against financial emergencies. This fund should ideally cover three to six months' worth of living expenses and be easily accessible in case of an unexpected expense or income disruption.

Savings Fund: Your savings fund, on the other hand, is more of a long-term savings vehicle, earmarked for specific goals or aspirations. This could include saving for a down payment on a home, a dream vacation, or a major life event like a wedding or college tuition.

Both types of funds are essential components of your financial toolkit and play complementary roles in your overall financial strategy.

3. Strategies for Building Emergency and Savings Funds

Now that we understand the importance of financial safety nets, let's talk about strategies for building emergency and savings funds. Building these funds requires discipline, consistency, and a commitment to prioritizing savings in your budget.

Start by setting specific savings goals for your emergency and savings funds. Determine how much you need to save for each fund and set a timeline for reaching your goals. Breaking down your goals into smaller, manageable milestones can make the process feel more achievable and keep you motivated along the way.

Next, automate your savings by setting up automatic transfers from your checking account to your emergency and savings accounts. Treat your savings like a non-negotiable expense, just like your mortgage payment or utility bill, and prioritize it accordingly.

Consider setting up separate accounts for your emergency and savings funds to keep them organized and easily accessible. High-yield savings accounts or money market accounts are ideal options for storing your emergency fund, as they offer liquidity and competitive interest rates.

4. The Power of Consistency and Discipline

Now that we've covered strategies for building emergency and savings funds, let's talk about the power of consistency and discipline in your savings journey. Consistency is key when it comes to building financial safety nets, as it allows you to make steady progress towards your goals over time.

Make saving a habit by incorporating it into your monthly budget as a non-negotiable expense. Treat your savings goals with the same level of importance as your other financial obligations, and make a commitment to prioritize them consistently.

But remember, building emergency and savings funds requires discipline and sacrifice. It may mean cutting back on non-essential expenses, finding ways to increase your income, or delaying gratification in favor of long-term financial security.

5. Leveraging Windfalls and Bonuses

Last but not least, let's talk about leveraging windfalls and bonuses to accelerate your savings goals. Windfalls—unexpected financial gains like tax refunds, bonuses, or inheritance—present an excellent opportunity to supercharge your emergency and savings funds and make significant strides towards your goals.

Instead of splurging on impulse purchases or lifestyle upgrades, consider allocating a portion of windfalls towards your savings goals. Whether it's contributing a lump sum to your emergency fund or jump-starting your savings fund, windfalls can provide a valuable boost to your financial progress.

But remember, it's essential to strike a balance between enjoying the present and preparing for the future. While it's tempting to spend windfalls on immediate gratification, investing in your financial security and long-term goals can ultimately bring greater satisfaction and peace of mind.

In conclusion, my fellow financial champions, building emergency and savings funds is the ultimate strategy for achieving financial resilience and accelerating your journey towards paying off your home loan faster. By prioritizing savings, automating your contributions, staying disciplined and consistent, and leveraging windfalls and bonuses, you'll build a solid financial foundation and unlock a world of endless possibilities.

So, what are you waiting for? It's time to roll up your sleeves, fortify your financial fortress, and pave the way towards homeownership success.

With each dollar you save and every milestone you reach, you're one step closer to realizing your dreams of mortgage freedom and financial security.

Here's to the extraordinary journey that awaits as you build emergency and savings funds and pave your own path towards financial success! Cheers to you and your unwavering commitment to achieving your goals!

CHAPTER 16

Part III: Cultivating Financial Discipline

Mastering Financial Discipline: The Key to Rapidly Paying Off Your Home Loan

Hey there, financial warriors! Are you ready to unlock the secret to paying off your home loan at lightning speed? Well, get ready to dive deep into the thrilling world of cultivating financial discipline—the ultimate superpower for achieving financial freedom and homeownership success!

1. Understanding the Power of Financial Discipline

Let's kick things off by shining a spotlight on the transformative power of financial discipline. Think of financial discipline as your secret weapon—a force that empowers you to make smart financial decisions, stay focused on your goals, and resist the temptations of impulse spending.

Financial discipline isn't just about saying "no" to unnecessary purchases or sticking to a budget—it's about cultivating habits and mindset that prioritize long-term financial success over short-term gratification. It's about making intentional choices with your money, setting clear goals, and staying committed to achieving them, no matter what obstacles may arise.

2. Setting Clear Financial Goals

Now that we've established the importance of financial discipline, let's talk about setting clear financial goals. Your goals are the compass that guides your financial journey, providing direction and purpose to your efforts. Whether it's paying off your home loan early, building an emergency fund, or saving for retirement, having clear goals gives you something to strive for and helps keep you motivated along the way.

Start by identifying your financial priorities and mapping out specific, measurable goals that align with your values and aspirations. Break down your goals into smaller, actionable steps and set deadlines for achieving them. This will help you stay focused and track your progress over time.

3. Creating and Sticking to a Budget

Now that we have our goals in place, let's talk about the cornerstone of financial discipline: creating and sticking to a budget. Your budget is your roadmap to financial success, outlining how much money you have coming in, where it's going, and how much you can afford to save and invest.

Start by tracking your income and expenses to get a clear picture of your financial situation. Identify areas where you can cut back on non-essential spending and allocate those savings towards your financial goals, like paying off your home loan faster.

But remember, a budget is only effective if you stick to it. This means resisting the urge to overspend, staying accountable to your goals, and making adjustments as needed to stay on track. It may require sacrifice and discipline in the short term, but the long-term benefits are well worth it.

4. Automating Your Finances

One of the best ways to maintain financial discipline is by automating your finances. Automating your savings, bill payments, and investments takes the guesswork out of managing your money and ensures that your financial goals are prioritized consistently.

Set up automatic transfers from your checking account to your savings or investment accounts to ensure that you're saving consistently each month. Use bill pay services or automatic payments to ensure that your bills are paid on time and avoid late fees.

Automating your finances not only helps you stay disciplined but also removes the temptation to spend money impulsively. By setting up automatic systems, you can focus your energy on other aspects of your life while your finances take care of themselves in the background.

5. Cultivating Healthy Financial Habits

Finally, let's talk about cultivating healthy financial habits that support your journey towards paying off your home loan fast. Financial discipline isn't just about following a budget or automating your finances—it's about adopting a mindset and lifestyle that prioritize financial health and well-being.

Start by practicing mindful spending and making intentional choices with your money. Before making a purchase, ask yourself if it aligns with your goals and if it's worth the cost. Consider implementing a "cooling-off" period for non-essential purchases to avoid impulse buying.

Next, prioritize saving and investing for the future. Make it a habit to save a portion of your income each month, even if it's just a small amount. Over time, these savings will add up and provide a cushion for emergencies or unexpected expenses.

Finally, educate yourself about personal finance and seek out resources and support to help you stay on track. Whether it's books, podcasts, or online communities, surrounding yourself with like-minded individuals who share your goals can provide motivation and accountability along your journey.

In conclusion, my fellow financial warriors, cultivating financial discipline is the ultimate key to paying off your home loan fast and achieving financial freedom. By setting clear goals, creating and sticking to a budget, automating your finances, and cultivating healthy financial habits, you'll build the foundation for a lifetime of financial success.

So, what are you waiting for? It's time to unleash your inner financial warrior, master the art of financial discipline, and pave the way towards homeownership success. With each choice you make and every step you take, you're one step closer to realizing your dreams of mortgage freedom and financial independence.

Here's to the extraordinary journey that awaits as you cultivate financial discipline and pave your own path towards financial success! Cheers to you and your unwavering commitment to achieving your goals!

CHAPTER 17

Crush Your Mortgage: The Ultimate Guide to Paying Off Your Home Loan Faster Than You Can Say "Cheddar Cheese"!

Hey there, fellow home loan warrior! Are you ready to embark on an epic journey to freedom from that pesky mortgage? Well, buckle up because we're about to dive into the thrilling world of developing a debt payoff strategy that will have you saying "sayonara" to that home loan faster than you can binge-watch a season of your favorite TV show!

Picture this: you wake up in the morning, stretch out like a cat, and realize something incredible—you're on the fast track to owning your home outright! No more shackles of debt holding you down, just the sweet taste of financial freedom.

Sounds pretty amazing, right? Well, my friend, it's not just a pipe dream. With the right plan and a sprinkle of determination, you can make it a reality.

Now, let's get down to business. Developing a debt payoff strategy is like crafting the perfect recipe for financial success. You need the right ingredients, a dash of discipline, and a pinch of patience. But fear not, because I'm here to guide you through every step of the way.

First things first, let's take a good hard look at your current financial situation. Whip out those spreadsheets (or open up your favorite budgeting app) and let's crunch some numbers. How much do you owe on your mortgage? What's your interest rate? And perhaps most importantly, how much extra cash can you throw at your loan each month?

Once you've got a clear picture of where you stand, it's time to start strategizing. One popular approach is the "debt snowball" method. Think of it like rolling a snowball down a hill—it starts off small, but as it picks up momentum, it becomes a unstoppable force. With the debt snowball method, you focus on paying off your smallest debts first, then snowballing those payments into tackling larger debts. It's a surefire way to build momentum and keep yourself motivated along the way.

Another option is the "debt avalanche" method. This strategy is all about tackling high-interest debt first, then working your way down to lower interest rates. It might not give you the same instant gratification as the debt snowball method, but it can save you a bundle in interest payments in the long run.

Of course, there's no one-size-fits-all approach to debt payoff. The key is to find a strategy that works for you and stick with it like glue. And remember, consistency is key! Even if you can only afford to throw an extra $50 towards your mortgage each month, every little bit helps.

Now, let's talk about some ninja-level tactics for supercharging your debt payoff journey. One sneaky trick is to make bi-weekly payments instead of monthly payments. By splitting your monthly payment in half and paying it every two weeks, you'll end up making an extra full payment each year without even breaking a sweat.

Another savvy move is to put any windfalls or unexpected cash—like tax refunds or birthday money—straight towards your mortgage. Sure, it might be tempting to blow it all on a fancy vacation or the latest tech gadget, but trust me, your future self will thank you for it.

And don't forget to keep an eye on interest rates! Refinancing your mortgage to snag a lower rate can potentially save you thousands of dollars over the life of your loan. It might seem like a hassle, but trust me, the payoff is more than worth it.

But perhaps the most important ingredient in your debt payoff recipe is patience. Rome wasn't built in a day, and neither will your mortgage be paid off overnight. It's a marathon, not a sprint, so don't get discouraged if you hit a few bumps in the road along the way.

So there you have it, my friend. With a solid plan, a sprinkle of discipline, and a whole lot of determination, you can crush your mortgage and reclaim your financial freedom once and for all. So go forth and conquer! The world is your oyster, and your mortgage is about to become ancient history.

Dispelling Mysteries in Debt Repayment: Your Ticket to a Mortgage-Free Future!

Hey there, savvy homeowner! Are you ready to crack the code on paying off your home loan faster than a cheetah on roller skates? Well, grab a seat and buckle up because we're about to embark on a wild ride through the world of debt repayment options. And trust me, it's going to be more fun than a barrel of monkeys!

Now, I know what you're thinking—debt repayment sounds about as thrilling as watching paint dry. But fear not, my friend, because I'm here to make it as entertaining as a circus act! So sit back, relax, and let's dive headfirst into the wonderful world of understanding your debt repayment options.

First things first, let's start by demystifying the different strategies you can use to pay off your home loan faster than you can say "supercalifragilisticexpialidocious." One popular option is the classic "debt snowball" method. It's like building a snowman—start with a tiny snowball (your smallest debt), then roll it around until it becomes a giant snow boulder (your mortgage). By focusing on paying off your smallest debts first and then snowballing those payments into tackling larger debts, you'll gain momentum faster than a downhill skier at the Winter Olympics.

But wait, there's more! If you're more of a math whiz than a snowball enthusiast, you might prefer the "debt avalanche" method. This strategy is all about tackling high-interest debt first, then working your way down to lower interest rates. It might not give you the same instant gratification as the debt snowball method, but it can save you a boatload of cash in interest payments in the long run. And who doesn't love saving money?

Of course, there's no one-size-fits-all approach to debt repayment. The key is to find a strategy that works for you and stick with it like glue. Whether you're a snowballer or an avalanche enthusiast, consistency is key! Even if you can only afford to throw an extra $20 towards your mortgage each month, every little bit helps.

134 | P a g e

Now, let's talk about some ninja-level tactics for supercharging your debt repayment journey. One sneaky trick is to make bi-weekly payments instead of monthly payments. By splitting your monthly payment in half and paying it every two weeks, you'll end up making an extra full payment each year without even breaking a sweat. It's like getting a bonus payment for free!

Another savvy move is to put any windfalls or unexpected cash—like tax refunds or birthday money—straight towards your mortgage. Sure, it might be tempting to blow it all on a fancy vacation or the latest tech gadget, but trust me, your future self will thank you for it. And who knows, maybe you'll even earn some extra brownie points with the universe for being so responsible!

But perhaps the most important ingredient in your debt repayment recipe is patience. Rome wasn't built in a day, and neither will your mortgage be paid off overnight. It's a marathon, not a sprint, so don't get discouraged if you hit a few bumps in the road along the way. Just keep chipping away at that debt like a sculptor carving a masterpiece out of marble, and before you know it, you'll be standing on top of the mountain shouting, "I'm debt-free!"

So there you have it, my friend. With a solid plan, a sprinkle of discipline, and a whole lot of determination, you can crush your mortgage and reclaim your financial freedom once and for all. So go forth and conquer! The world is your oyster, and your mortgage is about to become ancient history.

Battle of the Debt Titans: Debt Snowball vs. Debt Avalanche in the Quest for Mortgage Freedom!

Hey there, fellow financial adventurer! Are you ready to embark on an epic journey to slay the beast known as debt and conquer your mortgage faster than you can say "abracadabra"? Well, grab your sword (or calculator) because we're about to dive headfirst into the thrilling world of prioritizing debt repayment strategies. And trust me, it's going to be more exciting than a dragon-slaying quest!

Now, picture this: you wake up one morning, stretch out like a cat, and realize something incredible—you're on the fast track to owning your home outright! No more shackles of debt holding you down, just the sweet taste of financial freedom. Sounds pretty amazing, right? Well, buckle up, because we're about to uncover the two most powerful weapons in your debt-busting arsenal: the Debt Snowball and the Debt Avalanche.

First up, let's talk about the Debt Snowball. It's like building a snowman on a winter's day—start with a tiny snowball (your smallest debt), then roll it around until it becomes a giant snow boulder (your mortgage). With the Debt Snowball method, you focus on paying off your smallest debts first, then snowballing those payments into tackling larger debts. It's a surefire way to build momentum and keep yourself motivated along the way. Plus, who doesn't love the satisfaction of crossing off those smaller debts like a boss?

But hold onto your hats, because here comes the Debt Avalanche! This strategy is all about tackling high-interest debt first, then working your way down to lower interest rates. It might not give you the same instant gratification as the Debt Snowball method, but it can save you a boatload of cash in interest payments in the long run. It's like slaying the biggest, baddest dragon in the kingdom and reaping the rewards of your bravery.

So, which strategy is right for you? Well, that depends on your personality, financial situation, and goals. Are you the type of person who needs quick wins to stay motivated? Then the Debt Snowball might be your weapon of choice. Or maybe you're a math whiz who wants to minimize interest payments and maximize savings? In that case, the Debt Avalanche might be more up your alley.

But fear not, my friend, because no matter which strategy you choose, the key is to stick with it like glue. Consistency is key! Even if you can only afford to throw an extra $50 towards your mortgage each month, every little bit helps. And remember, Rome wasn't built in a day, and neither will your mortgage be paid off overnight. It's a marathon, not a sprint, so don't get discouraged if you hit a few bumps in the road along the way.

Now, let's talk about some ninja-level tactics for supercharging your debt repayment journey. One sneaky trick is to make bi-weekly payments instead of monthly payments. By splitting your monthly payment in half and paying it every two weeks, you'll end up making an extra full payment each year without even breaking a sweat. It's like getting a bonus payment for free!

Another savvy move is to put any windfalls or unexpected cash—like tax refunds or birthday money—straight towards your mortgage. Sure, it might be tempting to blow it all on a fancy vacation or the latest tech gadget, but trust me, your future self will thank you for it. And who knows, maybe you'll even earn some extra brownie points with the universe for being so responsible!

So there you have it, my friend. With the Debt Snowball and the Debt Avalanche by your side, you'll be well-equipped to conquer your mortgage and reclaim your financial freedom once and for all. So go forth and slay those debts like the fearless warrior you are! The kingdom of financial prosperity awaits, and your mortgage is about to become ancient history.

Conquer Your Mortgage Mountain with Avalanche Methods: The Ultimate Guide to Fast Home Loan Repayment!

Are you ready to embark on an epic adventure to slay the mortgage monster and claim victory over your home loan faster than a speeding bullet? Well, strap on your climbing gear and sharpen your ice axe, because we're about to scale the treacherous slopes of debt with Avalanche Methods, and trust me, it's going to be more exhilarating than a roller coaster ride!

So, what exactly are Avalanche Methods, you ask? Think of them as your trusty guide ropes, helping you navigate the perilous terrain of debt repayment with precision and efficiency. Unlike the Debt Snowball method, which focuses on paying off smaller debts first, Avalanche Methods take a more strategic approach, targeting high-interest debts with laser-like precision.

Picture this: you're standing at the base of a towering mountain—the summit of mortgage freedom looms high above, obscured by clouds of doubt and uncertainty. But fear not, because Avalanche Methods are here to help you conquer that mountain one step at a time.

The first step in your journey is to assess the lay of the land. How much do you owe on your mortgage? What's your interest rate? And perhaps most importantly, how much extra cash can you throw at your loan each month? Armed with this knowledge, you're ready to chart your course and begin your ascent.

Now, here's where the magic happens. With Avalanche Methods, you're going to focus all your firepower on the highest-interest debts first. These are the pesky little critters that are draining your bank account with their sky-high interest rates, so it's time to show them who's boss.

But wait, there's more! Avalanche Methods aren't just about throwing money at your debts willy-nilly. Oh no, they're about strategic planning and calculated strikes. You see, by targeting the highest-interest debts first, you're not only minimizing the amount of interest you'll pay over the long run, but you're also freeing up more cash to tackle those lower-interest debts later on.

It's like a game of financial chess, where every move is carefully calculated to maximize your chances of success. And trust me, when you see those high-interest debts start to crumble like a house of cards, you'll feel like the king (or queen) of the mountain!

But enough talk—let's get down to brass tacks. How exactly do you implement Avalanche Methods in your own debt repayment journey? Well, it's surprisingly simple. First, make a list of all your debts, sorted by interest rate from highest to lowest. Then, focus all your extra cash on paying off the highest-interest debt while making minimum payments on the rest.

As you chip away at that top debt, you'll start to see progress like never before. And once it's vanquished for good, you'll take all the money you were throwing at it and redirect it towards the next highest-interest debt on your list. Rinse and repeat until you've conquered them all!

But here's the best part: as you pay off each debt, you'll free up more and more cash to throw at the next one. It's like a snowball effect, but instead of building momentum with smaller debts, you're building momentum with strategic strikes against those high-interest behemoths.

Of course, no journey to the summit is without its challenges. There will be setbacks along the way— unexpected expenses, emergencies, maybe even a rogue blizzard or two. But fear not, because with Avalanche Methods in your toolkit, you'll be well-equipped to weather any storm that comes your way.

So there you have it, my friend. With Avalanche Methods as your trusty guide, you'll be well on your way to conquering your mortgage mountain and claiming victory over your home loan once and for all. So lace up those boots, grab your ice axe, and let's start climbing! The summit of financial freedom awaits, and with Avalanche Methods leading the way, you're sure to reach the top in record time.

Turbocharge Your Mortgage Payoff: Fun and Effective Strategies for Lightning-Speed Home Loan Repayment!

Unlock the secrets to turbocharging your mortgage payments and zipping past that finish line faster than a cheetah on a sugar rush? Well, buckle up and get ready for a wild ride, because we're about to dive into a treasure trove of fun and effective strategies that will have you saying "sayonara" to your home loan in no time!

First things first, let's set the stage. Picture this: you're lounging on your couch, sipping a cup of coffee, when suddenly it hits you like a bolt of lightning—you're tired of being shackled to that mortgage! But fear not, my friend, because with the right strategies in your arsenal, you'll be well-equipped to break free from the chains of debt and reclaim your financial freedom once and for all.

So, without further ado, let's jump right into the fun stuff: the strategies for accelerating your mortgage payments!

The Bi-Weekly Payment Trick: Who says you have to stick to the old-fashioned monthly payment schedule? With the bi-weekly payment trick, you'll make half of your monthly mortgage payment every two weeks. By doing this, you'll end up making an extra full payment each year without even breaking a sweat! It's like getting a bonus payment for free, and who doesn't love free money?

Round-Up Your Payments: Say goodbye to those pesky pennies and hello to round numbers! Every time you make a mortgage payment, round it up to the nearest hundred (or thousand, if you're feeling extra ambitious). It may not seem like much at first, but those little bits of extra cash will add up faster than you can say "cha-ching!"

Put Windfalls to Work: Did you just receive a tax refund? Or maybe a generous birthday gift from Aunt Mildred? Instead of blowing it all on a shopping spree, put that windfall to work by throwing it straight towards your mortgage. Trust me, your future self will thank you for it!

147 | P a g e

Refinance to Lower Rates: Keep an eye on interest rates and jump on the opportunity to refinance your mortgage if you can snag a lower rate. Not only will this potentially save you thousands of dollars over the life of your loan, but it'll also help you pay off your mortgage faster than you can say "interest savings!"

Channel Your Inner Side Hustler: Whether it's picking up a part-time job, freelancing on the side, or starting a small business, finding ways to increase your income can supercharge your mortgage payoff journey. Plus, who knows? You might discover a hidden talent or passion along the way!

Make Sacrifices (But Keep it Fun!): Okay, I know what you're thinking—sacrifices sound about as appealing as a root canal. But fear not, because with a little creativity, you can turn those sacrifices into fun challenges! Maybe it's a "no-spend" month where you challenge yourself to cook all your meals at home or a "DIY" month where you tackle home improvement projects instead of hiring out. Get creative and turn those sacrifices into opportunities for growth and adventure!

Celebrate Milestones: Paying off your mortgage is no small feat, so don't forget to celebrate the milestones along the way! Whether it's hitting a certain percentage paid off, reaching a specific dollar amount, or simply sticking to your accelerated payment plan for a certain length of time, take the time to pat yourself on the back and celebrate your progress. You've earned it!

So there you have it, my fellow mortgage mavens. With these fun and effective strategies in your toolkit, you'll be well on your way to accelerating your mortgage payments and reaching that finish line faster than you ever thought possible. So lace up those sneakers, put on your game face, and let's crush that mortgage like the financial rockstars we are!

CHAPTER 18

Mastering the Mortgage Marathon: A Playbook for Building Discipline, Setting Milestones, Overcoming Temptations, and Staying Motivated!

Hey there, mortgage mavens! Are you ready to embark on a thrilling adventure towards mortgage freedom? Well, grab your cape and tighten your shoelaces because we're about to dive into a whirlwind of strategies that will have you sprinting towards your home loan payoff faster than a superhero on a mission!

Building and Sustaining Discipline:

Alright, let's kick things off with the big D-word: Discipline. I know, I know, it's about as exciting as watching paint dry, but trust me, it's the secret sauce that will fuel your journey to mortgage freedom. So how do you build and sustain discipline when it comes to paying off your home loan?

First things first, set yourself up for success by creating a rock-solid budget. Take a good hard look at your income and expenses, and figure out exactly how much you can afford to throw at your mortgage each month. Then, stick to that budget like glue! Sure, it might mean cutting back on those fancy lattes or skipping out on that impulse shopping spree, but trust me, your future self will thank you for it.

Next, automate your payments whenever possible. Set up automatic transfers from your bank account to your mortgage lender so you never have to worry about missing a payment. It's like putting your finances on autopilot and freeing up valuable brain space for more important things, like binge-watching your favorite TV show or perfecting your avocado toast recipe.

And finally, find an accountability buddy to keep you on track. Whether it's a friend, family member, or even a furry companion, having someone to cheer you on and hold you accountable can make all the difference. Plus, who doesn't love a little friendly competition?

Setting Clear Financial Milestones:

Alright, now that you've got your discipline game on lock, it's time to set some clear financial milestones to keep you motivated along the way. Think of them as little checkpoints on your journey to mortgage freedom, each one bringing you closer and closer to the finish line.

Start by setting a specific payoff date for your mortgage. Maybe it's five years from now, ten years from now, or heck, even next year if you're feeling extra ambitious! Whatever date you choose, make sure it's realistic and achievable based on your current financial situation.

Next, break down that big goal into smaller, bite-sized milestones. Maybe it's paying off a certain percentage of your mortgage, reaching a specific dollar amount, or hitting a certain number of consecutive on-time payments. Whatever it is, make sure it's something you can celebrate along the way and use as motivation to keep pushing forward.

And don't forget to reward yourself when you hit those milestones! Whether it's treating yourself to a fancy dinner, splurging on a little indulgence, or simply giving yourself a pat on the back, taking the time to acknowledge your progress will keep you motivated and inspired to keep pushing forward.

Overcoming Temptations and Impulse Spending:

Alright, let's talk about the elephant in the room: Temptations and impulse spending. We've all been there—you walk past your favorite coffee shop and suddenly find yourself shelling out $5 for a fancy latte, or you see that shiny new gadget on sale and before you know it, it's in your shopping cart.

But fear not, my friend, because with a little bit of self-awareness and a few clever tricks up your sleeve, you can overcome those temptations and keep your spending in check.

First, take a good hard look at your spending habits and identify any areas where you tend to splurge. Maybe it's dining out too often, indulging in retail therapy, or subscribing to every streaming service known to mankind. Once you've identified those trouble spots, come up with a plan to combat them. Maybe it's setting a strict monthly spending limit, unsubscribing from unnecessary services, or finding cheaper alternatives to your favorite indulgences.

Next, practice the art of delayed gratification. Instead of giving in to those impulse purchases right away, give yourself a cooling-off period to think it over. Maybe it's waiting 24 hours before pulling the trigger on that new gadget or asking yourself if you really need that fancy latte before handing over your hard-earned cash. You'd be surprised how often you'll find yourself realizing you can live without that impulse purchase after all.

And finally, surround yourself with like-minded individuals who share your financial goals and values. Whether it's joining a support group, finding a buddy to hold you accountable, or simply following inspiring accounts on social media, having a strong support system can make all the difference when it comes to staying on track with your financial goals.

Staying Motivated Through Challenges:

Alright, let's be real for a second—paying off your mortgage is no walk in the park. There will be challenges along the way, setbacks, and moments of doubt. But fear not, because with the right mindset and a few clever tricks, you can stay motivated and keep pushing forward no matter what life throws your way.

First and foremost, remember why you started this journey in the first place. Whether it's achieving financial freedom, owning your home outright, or simply proving to yourself that you can do it, keep that end goal front and center in your mind at all times. Visualize yourself standing on the other side of that mortgage, basking in the glow of your hard-earned success, and let that vision fuel your fire.

Next, break up your journey into smaller, more manageable chunks. Instead of focusing on the daunting task of paying off your entire mortgage, focus on smaller, bite-sized goals that you can achieve one step at a time. Maybe it's making it through the month without blowing your budget, hitting a certain percentage paid off, or simply sticking to your accelerated payment plan for a certain length of time. Whatever it is, celebrate those small victories along the way and use them as fuel to keep pushing forward.

And finally, don't be afraid to ask for help when you need it. Whether it's reaching out to your support system for words of encouragement, seeking advice from a financial advisor, or simply venting your frustrations to a sympathetic ear, remember that you're not in this alone. We're all in this together, and together, we can conquer any challenge that comes our way.

So there you have it, my fellow mortgage mavens. With discipline, clear financial milestones, strategies for overcoming temptations, and a healthy dose of motivation, you'll be well on your way to paying off your home loan faster than you ever thought possible. So lace up those boots, put on your game face, and let's crush that mortgage like the financial rockstars we are!

Conclusion

Unleash Your Mortgage-Free Future!

Congratulations, dear reader, you've made it to the final chapter of our journey together—a journey filled with insight, empowerment, and the promise of a brighter financial future. As we bid farewell to the pages of this book, let's take a moment to reflect on the incredible adventure we've embarked upon, and the valuable lessons we've learned along the way.

From understanding the intricacies of the home loan journey to unraveling the importance of paying off your mortgage early, we've laid the groundwork for success. We've debunked common challenges and misconceptions, armed with knowledge to navigate the twists and turns of the financial landscape.

In Part I, we delved into the world of maximizing income streams, exploring additional sources of revenue and leveraging side hustles for financial growth. Whether it's freelancing, property investments, or cultivating passive income streams, we've unlocked the doors to new opportunities and expanded our financial horizons.

In Part II, we turned our attention to budgeting and financial management, creating comprehensive budget plans, trimming expenses, and increasing savings. We've learned the art of tracking expenses, setting realistic goals, and prioritizing debt repayment, all while building emergency funds and securing our financial future.

And in Part III, we honed our financial discipline, developing debt payoff strategies, setting clear milestones, and overcoming temptations and impulse spending. With unwavering determination and resilience, we've faced challenges head-on, staying motivated and inspired on our journey to mortgage freedom.

As we close the final chapter of this book, remember that the power to shape your financial destiny lies within your hands. Armed with the knowledge, skills, and strategies outlined within these pages, you possess the tools to transform your dreams into reality.

So go forth, dear reader, and unleash your mortgage-free future! Let the lessons learned and insights gained serve as your guiding light on the path to financial independence and prosperity. With courage, determination, and a sprinkle of creativity, there's no limit to what you can achieve.

Thank you for joining me on this incredible adventure. May your journey be filled with abundance, success, and the joy of realizing your dreams. Here's to a future brimming with possibilities, and to the exciting chapters yet to be written. Until we meet again, happy reading, and may your mortgage-free future be brighter than ever before!